The English Job Interview

The English Job Interview

Published by
The Yeungnam University Press
2021

214-1, Gyeongsan City, Gyeongsangbuk-do
(Tel) 053-810-1801-4 (Fax) 053-810-4722
http://book.yu.ac.kr

First Published
30th August 2021

ISBN 978-89-7581-844-8 13740

The English Job Interview

Alex Johnson | Tiffany Ballard

Yeungnam University Press

CONTENTS

UNIT 1

JOBS, GOALS, AND PERCEPTIONS

LET'S GET TO KNOW EACH OTHER!

You are going to meet and talk to three new classmates. Ask the questions and write SHORT answers in the boxes. We will use the answers to get to know each other.

Question	Student 1	Student 2	Student 3
Nice to meet you! What's your name?			
What's your major?			
What year are you in school?			
Have you ever had a part-time job? (If yes) Where did you work? What did you do?			
Have you ever done any volunteer work? (If yes) What did you do?			
How long have you studied English? Will English help you find a job? (Yes/No) Why?			
What are some popular jobs for young people these days? (Make a list)			
Have you ever had a job interview? Explain			
What job do you want in the future? Why?			

GETTING STARTED: MY GOAL

On your own: make a list of jobs you would like to do

With your partner or group, discuss these questions:

- What do you know about these jobs?
- Why do you want to do these jobs?
- What kind of skills do you need to do these jobs?

On your own: make a list of companies you would like to work for

With your partner or group, discuss these questions:

- What do you know about these companies?
- Why do you want to work for these companies?
- Where are these companies located?
- What industry are they in? If you don't know, guess.

JOBS

Vocabulary / Job Duties

Think of other jobs you know: Write the job and the duties

Job Type:	Job Duties:
Government Officer	Help the public / follow government rules and regulations
Flight Attendant	Guide and assist passengers
Banker	
Barista	

JOBS AND PERCEPTION

Name three jobs for each category. Add any more vocabulary that you might know.

High-salaried			
Exciting			
Uninteresting			
Prestigious			
Popular			
Difficult			
Stable			
Low-salaried			

Explain why these jobs fit into each category. You may have different thoughts than your partners.

I think ········ is uninteresting because·····························.

WHAT WOULD YOU LIKE IN A JOB?

Job satisfaction is the feeling of pleasure and achievement you have while doing your job. You will express your opinions with your partner or group about situations you might have in the future.

Opinions:
I agree
I disagree
It doesn't matter
I don't know

I only want to work in the Daegu area.	I don't want to get a job where I travel a lot.	Working overtime is ok for me.
I only want to work regular hours. (example 8 to 5)	I only want to work in an office.	I want to wear a suit or uniform at work.
I want to have a lot of responsibility	Salary is the most important thing for me.	Opportunities for advancement are very important.
I don't want to be stuck behind a desk.	My co-workers are a very important part of work.	I like to work alone.

Make a list of five important things for you to be satisfied with your future job. Discuss them with your partner or your group.

1. ______________________________
2. ______________________________
3. ______________________________
4. ______________________________
5. ______________________________

CRITICAL THINKING

1. What are some ways to improve your chances of getting the job you want in the future?
2. From the jobs we've discussed so far on pages 7, 8, and 9, which of the jobs might you want to do, and what jobs would you definitely NOT want to do? Explain to your partner or group.
3. Have you ever had a part-time job? What was the best part? What was the worst part? Explain. What skills did you learn that you could use in the future?
4. What was your dream job when you were a child? Explain. Do you still want this job now? Explain
5. What kind of skills do you need for the job(s) you want?
6. Make your own questions!

UNIT 2

JOB SEARCH AND APPLICATIONS

JOB APPLICATIONS

These days, most job applications are done online. However, sometimes you might be asked to fill in a paper application.

Fill out the job application on the following two pages.

If there is anything that doesn't apply to you, the standard is to write "N/A" in the blank space.

> Example: If you have never had a job, in the section "FORMER EMPLOYERS" you would write "N/A" and then move on to the next section.

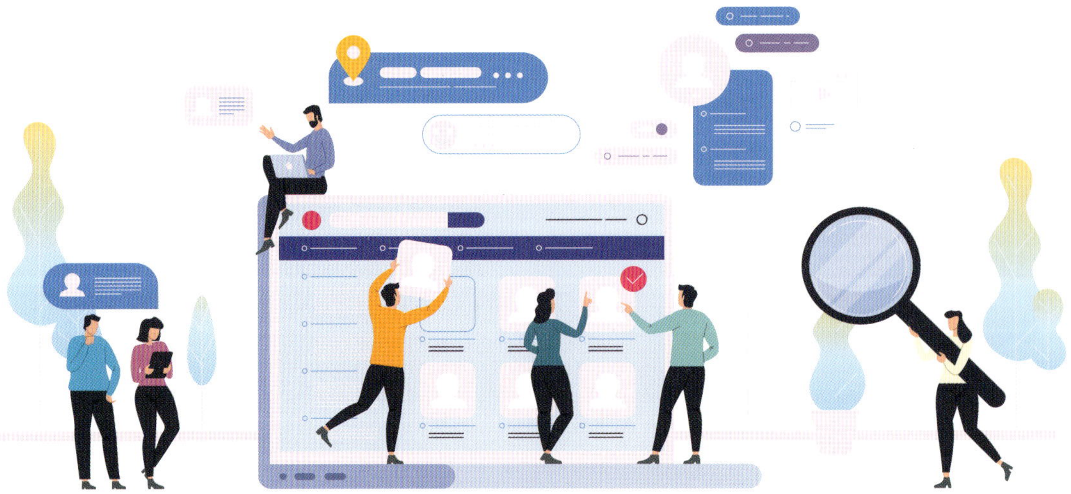

FORMER EMPLOYERS *List below current and last three employers, starting with most recent one first. Please include any non-paid/volunteer experience which is related to the job for which you are applying. Please complete even if you attach a resume.*

Date (M/D/Y)

	Date (M/D/Y)	Employer	Salary Or Hourly	Position	Reason For Leaving
1	From To	Current Employer (Name and Address of Employer - Type of Business)	Starting ______ Ending ______ If hourly, average # of hours per week ______		
	Duties Performed				
	Supervisor's Name		Phone Number		May We Contact?
2	From To	Previous Employer (Name and Address of Employer - Type of Business)	Starting ______ Ending ______ If hourly, average # of hours per week ______		
	Duties Performed				
	Supervisor's Name		Phone Number		May We Contact?
3	From To	Previous Employer (Name and Address of Employer - Type of Business)	Starting ______ Ending ______ If hourly, average # of hours per week ______		
	Duties Performed				
	Supervisor's Name		Phone Number		May We Contact?
4	From To	Previous Employer (Name and Address of Employer - Type of Business)	Starting ______ Ending ______ If hourly, average # of hours per week ______		
	Duties Performed				
	Supervisor's Name		Phone Number		May We Contact?

REFERENCES *Give below the names of three professional references, whom you have known at least one year.*

Name	Address & Phone Number	Business	Years Acquainted How Do You Know This Person?
1			
2			
3			

I hereby authorize Starbucks to thoroughly investigate my background, references, employment record and other matters related to my suitability for employment. I authorize persons, schools, my current employer (if applicable), and previous employers and organizations contacted by Starbucks to provide any relevant information regarding my current and/or previous employment and I release all persons, schools, employers of any and all claims for providing such information. I understand that misrepresentation or omission of facts may result in rejection of this application, or if hired, discipline up to and including dismissal. I understand that I may be required to sign a confidentiality and/or non-compete agreement, should I become an employee of Starbucks Coffee Company. I understand that nothing contained in this application, or conveyed during any interview which may be granted, is intended to create an employment contract. I understand that filling out this form does not indicate there is a position open and does not obligate Starbucks to hire me. ***(U.S. APPLICANTS ONLY: I understand and agree that my employment is at will, which means that it is for no specified period and may be terminated by me or Starbucks at any time without prior notice for any reason. MARYLAND APPLICANTS ONLY: Under Maryland law, an employer may not require or demand, as a condition of employment, prospective employment, or continued employment, that an individual submit to or take, a lie detector or similar test. An employer who violates this law is guilty of misdemeanor and subject to a fine not exceeding $100. MASSACHUSETTS APPLICANTS ONLY: It is unlawful in Massachusetts to require or administer a lie detector test as a condition of employment or continued employment. An employer who violates this law shall be subject to criminal penalties and civil liability. CALIFORNIA APPLICANTS ONLY: Applicant may omit any convictions for the possession of marijuana (except for convictions for the possessions of marijuana on school grounds or possession of concentrated cannabis) that are more than two(2) years old, and any information concerning a referral to, and participation in, any pretrial or post trial diversion program.***

Date____________________ Signature____________________

For Retail positions please submit this application at your nearest store location. For non-retail openings, please visit our website at www.starbucks.com to apply for any posted position.

WE ARE AN EQUAL OPPORTUNITY EMPLOYER COMMITTED TO HIRING A DIVERSE WORKFORCE.

PRINTED ON RECYCLED PAPER

APPLICATION FOR EMPLOYMENT

Starbucks Coffee Company is an equal opportunity employer, dedicated to a policy of non-discrimination in employment on any basis including race, color, age, sex, religion, national origin, the presence of mental, physical, or sensory disability, sexual orientation, or any other basis prohibited by federal, state, or provincial law.

Please complete entire application to ensure processing.

PERSONAL INFORMATION (Please print)

Name Last First Middle Social Security/Social Insurance Number Date (M/D/Y)

Other names you are known by ____________ Are you less than 18 years of age? Yes____ No____ (Starbucks is required to comply with federal, state, or provincial law.)

U.S. Applicant Only:
Are you legally eligible for employment in the U.S.? Yes______ No______
(All new hires will be required to provide proof of eligibility to work in the U.S.)

Have you been convicted of a crime in the last seven (7) years? Yes____ No____
If Yes, list convictions that are a matter of public record (arrests are not convictions). A conviction will not necessarily disqualify you for employment.

Present Address Street City State/Province Zip Code/Postal Code

Permanent Address Street City State/Province Zip Code/Postal Code

Phone Number Daytime Evening Referred By

EMPLOYMENT DESIRED (if you are applying for a retail hourly position, please keep in mind that the availability of hours may vary.)

Position Location/Department Salary Desired Date You Can Start

Specify hours available for each day of the week	Sunday	Monday	Tuesday	Wednesday	Thursday	Friday	Saturday

Are you able to work overtime?__________
Have you ever worked for Starbucks Coffee Company?_________ If yes, when? _____________ Which store/department?____________________

EDUCATION

	Name and Address of School	Circle Last Years Completed	Did You Graduate?	Subjects Studied and Degrees Received
High School		1 2 3 4	Y N	
College		1 2 3 4	Y N	
Post College		1 2 3 4	Y N	
Trade, Business, or Correspondence School		1 2 3 4	Y N	

List skills relevant to the position applied for____

SKILLS *For Office/Administrative positions only* Typing WPM:__________________ 10-Key: ☐ Yes ☐ No

Computer Proficiency: ☐ Word for Windows ☐ Excel ☐ Others: ______________________________

Have you ever visited a Starbucks Coffee location? Where? Describe your experience. ____________________________
____
____

What do you like about coffee?____
____

Why would you like to work for Starbucks Coffee Company?_______________________________
____
____

Describe a specific situation where you have provided excellent customer service in your most recent position. Why was this effective? ____________
____
____

SKU #193822

wondershare

SEARCHING FOR A JOB

Look at the vocabulary and circle good ways to find a job.

Internet job sites	Use search engines	Speaking with friends and relatives
School career center	Network with people who work in that field	Internships
Search company websites	Attend a job fair	Headhunters

Choose the top five and put them in order from MOST to LEAST effective.

____

____

____

____

____

Explain your answers to your partner or group.

USING "KEYWORDS" FOR JOB SEARCHES

The internet has become the most common way for people to find available jobs. When we search, we need to use "keywords." Keywords are the words that match the available jobs you are interested in.

Example: You want to be a TEACHER.

You can search for the word TEACHER, but you can also search keywords like PRIMARY EDUCATION, DAEGU, FULL-TIME

Some terms aren't the same in English as they are in Korean. Be careful! Ex: "Ground crew" has a very different meaning in each language.

Different categories of keywords include:

Field or industry	banking, hospitality, retail, healthcare, media, etc.
Company names	Starbucks, Samsung, Kia, etc.
Location	Seoul, California, South Korea, UAE
Job type	Full-time, part-time, contract, freelance, consultant, etc.
Desired job title	Manager, director, programmer, head chef, accountant, entry level, etc.
Specific industry skills	computer programming language (JAVA), certifications (TESOL), degrees (PhD)

Think of three jobs you are interested in (you can look back at Unit 1) and write five keywords that you could use in a search.

JOB KEYWORDS

________________ ____

________________ ____

________________ ____

TOP JOB SEARCH WEBSITES

Brainstorm the top FOUR websites to look for jobs in Korea.

____

____

____

____

____

These are the top FOUR websites to look for jobs in English in the U.S.

Indeed.com
Monster.com
Simplyhired.com
CareerBuilder.com

IN CLASS ACTIVITY

Choose one Korean website and one English website and search for jobs you are interested in. Be sure to use keywords in your search!

HOMEWORK

Find TWO current job postings (in English), print both, and bring them to the next class. It doesn't have to be a job you're personally interested in, and can be from any industry.

Look at your partner's job posting
See if you can find the following information

Name of company:	
Job title:	
Location of job:	
Contact information: (may include telephone number, e-mail address, person's name, department name)	
Opening and closing dates of the job / deadline:	
Salary:	
Responsibilities:	
Education requirements:	
Qualifications:	
Relevant work experience needed:	

Look at your partner's job posting
See if you can find the following information

Name of company:	
Job title:	
Location of job:	
Contact information: (may include telephone number, e-mail address, person's name, department name)	
Opening and closing dates of the job / deadline:	
Salary:	
Responsibilities:	
Education requirements:	
Qualifications:	
Relevant work experience needed:	

UNIT 3

WRITING RESUMES

· What is a resume?

A resume is a brief, concise document that presents your most relevant and positive credentials for employment, admission to graduate school, consideration for a scholarship or fellowship, or other professional purpose.

· What should a resume include?

A resume needs to include

- **Personal information:** Name, contact information
- **Education:** Schools you attended, certificates, and other things you have learned
- **Work Experience: ANY** and **ALL** work you have done (full-time, part-time, volunteer)

A resume needs to have your information in a clear and easy format so an employer can quickly see your personal information, education, and work experience.
You must pay attention to every small detail in formatting. Recruiters and hiring managers are judging you on your <u>attention to detail</u>.

***A recruiter spends only 6 seconds scanning a resume!**

· How do you write a resume?

1. Look at sample resumes online or in books

2. Use a resume template (a computer program that helps you format your information) MS-Word has free templates and there are many online. https://templates.office.com/en-us/Resumes-and-Cover-Letters You need to find a resume template that works for your goals and background.

ANALYZE A RESUME

Fill in the answers for the resume on the next page

What is the applicant's first and last name?	First: ____________
	Last: ____________
What is her current address?	____________
What is her telephone number?	____________
What is her e-mail address?	____________
What is her major?	____________
When will she graduate from university?	____________
What is her current job?	____________
Does she have any volunteer experience?	____________
What kind of skills does she have?	____________
What jobs has she had?	____________

***A PART-TIME JOB IS CONSIDERED JOB EXPERIENCE!**

JI HYE KIM

123 Daehak-ro, Gyeongsan, Gyeongbuk 38555, South Korea
+82 10-1234-5678
Jihyekim2001@gmail.com

EXPERIENCE

MARCH 2017 - CURRENT
TEACHER
KID'S CAMPUS ENGLISH ACADEMY

- Developed teamwork by sharing teaching ideas with colleagues
- Designed content to fit individual student needs
- Created all materials such as making my own exam questions

FEBRUARY 2016 - AUGUST 2016
ADMINISTRATIVE ASSISTANCE
OFFICE OF THE YEUNGNAM UNIVERSITY REGISTRAR

- Increased office's work efficiency by organizing documents
- Coordinated with other departments

FEBRUARY 2015 - DECEMBER 2015
CASHIER & BARISTA
EDIYA COFFEE

- Cooperated with team members
- Mastered pos system
- Dealt with customer complaints promptly and effectively

EDUCATION

YEUNGNAM UNIVERSITY- GYEONGSAN, SOUTH KOREA
B.A., English Language and Literature
March 2015 - Graduation Expected: December 2019
Studied courses in English literature, speaking, writing and communication

UNIVERSITY OF NEBRASKA AT OMAHA - OMAHA, NE, USA
Exchange Student Program
August 2016 - December 2016
Studied courses in English speaking, writing and service learning

CERTIFICATES

TOEIC 950 & TOEIC SPEAKING Lv.7
MS Office certificate

WORKSHEET: PREPARING THE INFORMATION FOR YOUR RESUME

First name: ______________________

Last name: ______________________

Address: ____

Telephone number: ______________________________________

E-mail: ____

Education: (School, major, expected graduation date)

____

____

Work Experience: (Full-time, part-time, volunteer - include months and years)

____

____

____

Skills:

____

____

____

WHAT ARE THE BEST WAYS TO SHOW YOUR SKILLS ON A RESUME?

We usually think of skills in two different types:

HARD SKILLS (quantifiable)	Proficiency in a language (like a test score), computer languages, operating a machine, certificates, etc.
SOFT SKILLS (interpersonal)	teamwork, flexibility, patience, time management, communication, persuasion, etc.

Hard skills can be listed on your resume.

Soft skills need to be demonstrated with specific examples through any work experience or volunteer experience you've had.

Look back at the previous sample resume. What are the person's HARD skills and SOFT skills? How are the soft skills demonstrated?

HARD	SOFT
______________________	______________________
______________________	______________________
______________________	______________________
______________________	______________________

KEYWORDS:
How to decide which skills to highlight in your resume

Job recruiters spend on average only 6 seconds scanning your resume, and sometimes, a computer program will screen your resume for specific keywords.

Use the job posting and the company's "About us" page on their website to find keywords to include in your resume. DO NOT COPY any part of their writing, but rather, focus on words/qualities that you see multiple times. This can be a clue as to what they're really looking for.

Here is an example of a job posting:

Alaska Airlines
Customer Service Agent - Full Time in Seattle, Washington

WHAT WE'RE ABOUT

We're creating an airline people love. It begins with each Alaska Airlines employee, bringing unique strengths and energy to our work in the air and on the ground. Every day, we go beyond what's expected and reach for the remarkable, together.

POSITION INFORMATION

Role Summary: The Customer Services Agent (CSA) works in a fast-paced environment assisting customers with travel needs, such as answering inquiries, ticketing, checking-in passengers, and boarding flights.

Key Duties

- Assists customers with travel needs (e.g., answering inquiries, ticketing, checking-in passengers, and boarding flights) in a fast-paced environment.
- Sells tickets and ensures cabin accommodations.
- Performs computer and paperwork tasks.
- Evaluates and prepares flights by arranging seat assignments and load, coordinating special meals, and upgrades.
- Performs boarding and gate duties (e.g., checking flight tickets, assisting and directing passengers, making announcements, checking aircraft, and confirming cabin security).
- Operates, including driving, jet bridge.
- Processes and secures passenger luggage.
- At the direction of management, may be assigned to perform duties of varying capacities to ensure complete customer satisfaction.

Job-Specific Skills Required

- A minimum of 2 years of customer service or community service experience.
- Possess exceptional interpersonal and communication skills (e.g., verbal, written, listening).
- Typing speed of at least 25 WPM.
- Flexibility to work varied shifts (e.g., weekends, holidays).
- Ability to participate in paid training.

Alaska Airlines
Customer Service Agent - Full Time in Seattle, Washington

- Ability and willingness to accept a starting pay of $10.72 per hour (may vary depending on location).
- Ability to learn and operate a computerized reservation system.
- Ability to adapt to performing work according to set procedures.
- Ability to anticipate needs of others in a fast paced environment.
- Must have a valid Driver's license and Current Passport or Enhanced Driver's license at time of hire.
- Minimum age of 18.
- Must be authorized to work in the U.S.

Job-Specific Leadership Expectations

- Embody our values to own safety, do the right thing, be kind-hearted, deliver performance, and be remarkable.

Education

- High school diploma or equivalent is required.

Submit your application by 01/03/2019 11:59pm (Pacific Time).
We'll be happy to see it.

Job ID: 33097
Location: Seattle, WA
Full/Part Time: Full-Time
Regular/Temporary: Regular

ANALYZE THE JOB POSTING

You can see all the clues provided by the potential employer. What hard skills are they looking for? What soft skills are they looking for?

DISCUSS WITH YOUR PARTNER

Make a list of the hard skills and soft skills they are looking for in the job posting.

HARD SKILLS	**SOFT SKILLS**

What skills do you have that match this job posting?

*Have you done any part-time jobs where you helped customers? If so, you might match some of the qualifications, like "Assist customers" listed under Key Duties, depending on your experiences.

ANALYZE THE JOB POSTING

When you're writing your resume, think about the skills that they are looking for that match your skills.

For example, if you worked at CGV, you can show your relevant skills on your resume that match the following qualifications from this job posting.

- ▶ "Sells tickets and ensures cabin accommodations" = Sold tickets and ensured customers find their correct seats
- ▶ "Assists customers with travel needs…in a fast paced environment" = Assisted customers with discounts and coupons in a fast paced environment

***Once you know what skills they're looking for, you can write your resume to try to match those skills!**

Example for a resume

CGV Team Member
August 2017-December 2018

- Resolved ticketing problems for customers with kiosk ticketing machine
- Sold tickets and ensured customers find their correct seats
- Coordinated and arranged movie poster displays
- Assisted customers with discounts and coupons in a fast paced environment

PRACTICE: Analyze your job posting

Go through your job posting carefully. List the hard skills and soft skills they are looking for

HARD SKILLS	**SOFT SKILLS**

Now, choose at least three specific skills that they are looking for that match skills that you have. Write some ideas for your own resume here!

____

____

____

ACTIVITY: POWER WORDS
ACTIVE VERBS MAKE ALL THE DIFFERENCE

You want to really highlight your achievements and accomplishments. The best way to do that is to use POWER WORDS to make your resume "stand out from the crowd."

Here are some helpful POWER WORDS

Produced	Directed	Resolved
Coordinated	Mentored	Created
Organized	Supervised	Encouraged
Designed	Developed	Increased

Instead of writing this:

Starbucks Barista: Sept 2017 - Aug 2018

- Changed the display for the coffee

You can write this:

Starbucks Barista: Sept 2017 - Aug 2018

- Designed displays for new coffee products, which increased sales by 15%

Find the POWER WORDS in the resume on the next page!

MIN SU KIM

| (+82)10-1234-5678 | MinSuKim@gmail.com

EXPERIENCE

Nov.2018~May.2019 Barista, Mosaic Café
- Enhanced problem-solving skills by resolving customer problems
- Created new coffee drinks and desserts
- Assisted customers in a fast paced environment

Aug.2017~Nov.2018 Restaurant Server, Black Angus Steakhouse
- Developed teamwork skills by collaborating with colleagues
- Improved communication skills by dealing with customers
- Contributed to high sales and promotions

Feb.2017~Aug.2017 Internship program , USAG Daegu
- Advanced knowledge of computer programming
- Mentored kids with proficient language skills
- Increased work efficiency by submitting daily report

July.2016~July.2016 Volunteer, Daegu Chi-Mec Festival
- Spearheaded program for other volunteers
- Collaborated with different organizations

EDUCATION

2015.03~Graduation expected: 2021.02 B.A. ENGLISH LANGUAGE AND LITERATURE
YEUNGNAM UNIVERSITY

TEST & CERTIFICATES

TOEIC 905 / OPIC speaking test AL
ms office

ASSIGNMENT 1: RESUME

1. Chose a template that works for your goals and background.
2. Make sure your skills are demonstrated by using POWER WORDS
3. Print ________ copies and bring them to class on Peer Workshop Day.

Peer Workshop Day - first draft due: ________________

Final draft due: ________________

RESUME: PEER WORKSHOP

Peer Edited by: (student)	Excellent	Good	Needs improvement	Comments
Appearance/Style Is the resume visually appealing?				
Completeness/Length Is the resume complete, but not too long or too short?				
Content/Layout Does the resume have sections such as • Name and contact info • Education • Awards or certificates • Experience • Activities/Volunteering • Other?				
Editing/Grammar Is the resume free of errors? What changes/edits need to be made?				
Use of keywords/action verbs Does the resume include keywords from the job posting? Does it use action verbs or POWER WORDS?				
Details Check and double check ALL fine details of formatting etc.				

RESUME: PEER WORKSHOP

Peer Edited by: ______ (student)	Excellent	Good	Needs improvement	Comments
Appearance/Style Is the resume visually appealing?				
Completeness/Length Is the resume complete, but not too long or too short?				
Content/Layout Does the resume have sections such as • Name and contact info • Education • Awards or certificates • Experience • Activities/Volunteering • Other?				
Editing/Grammar Is the resume free of errors? What changes/edits need to be made?				
Use of keywords/action verbs Does the resume include keywords from the job posting? Does it use action verbs or POWER WORDS?				
Details Check and double check ALL fine details of formatting etc.				

UNIT 4

WRITING A COVER LETTER

What is a cover letter?

- A cover **letter** is an introduction letter that highlights your strong points and gives the company a first impression of you. This letter is meant to ***intrigue*** a potential employer. You have an opportunity to "***sell yourself***" in a cover letter. While the resume is a list of facts, the cover letter allows you to show your personality and your writing skills

- A cover letter usually has the following parts:
  - ✓ Header 1
  - ✓ Greeting 2
  - ✓ Introduction 3
  - ✓ Body 4
  - ✓ Closing5
  - ✓ Signature 6

Just like the resume, we can use a template to help us format our cover letter.

If you used a specific template for your resume, try to find/use the matching one for your cover letter. Otherwise, use a "basic" cover letter template.

Look at the following sample cover letter 1. **Find and label the different parts.**

SAMPLE COVER LETTER: 1

Jane Jones

Daelim Apt 202/1234
Duho-dong, Buk-gu
Pohang-si, South Korea
+82 10-1234-5678

Including your address is optional

Dear Hiring Manager,

I am writing to express my interest in the flight attendant position at Singapore Airlines, which I heard about from a friend who is a current employee. Because of my enthusiasm and interpersonal skills, I am confident that I would be a great fit for your cabin crew.

My work experience as a translator and cultural ambassador through my university's buddy program helped me develop patience and understanding of different cultures. I helped students adapt to Korean academic and social life. I also maintained a successful relationship with students after the program.

My passion for communicating in English was ignited while traveling to different countries. Socializing with people from different countries and learning about their cultures was not only interesting, but also enabled me to gain an understanding of diversity. Furthermore, my memories with lifelong friends from Italy, Mexico, and other places continue to inspire me to not be afraid to try new things.

I would love the opportunity to speak with you further about the position. Thank you for your consideration and I look forward to hearing from you.

Sincerely,

Jane Jones
janejones@gmail.com

TIPS FOR WRITING A GREAT COVER LETTER

Greeting:

Make sure you have the correct name of the person you're sending the letter to. If the job posting lists the name of a person, <u>then use that</u>. If not, you can address the letter to the head of the appropriate department you are applying to. You can also check the company's website for a "contact" or "about us" page to find out who is doing the hiring.

◈ As a last option, you can use "Dear Hiring Manager"

- Dear Mr./Ms. [Last name] is the most common in business, but if you aren't sure if it's a man or a woman, use Dear [First name] [Last name]
- Do not use "To whom it may concern." This is old fashioned and gives a bad first impression that you were too lazy to try find the person's name.

Introduction:

Your first few sentences usually serve as a short introduction, what position you're applying for, and why you think this job is a good match for your talents.

Example:

- I am interested in ____________ (job) at __________ (company).
- I was excited to see that ________ (company) is looking to hire a/an _______________ (job title).
- I am writing to express my interest in the _____________________

Body:

Show them what you can do! Instead of saying why you want the job, try to take the approach of "Here's why you want ME to work for YOU."

- Tell them why you are the best person for the job
- Highlight your skills (ex: language, customer service, sales,….)
- Focus on keywords from the job posting
- Don't simply restate what's on your resume; instead provide specific examples that demonstrate your abilities
- Make sure your letter isn't generic (Boring)

Closing:

The closing finishes the letter and encourages the hiring manager to contact you.

Examples:

- I would love the opportunity to speak with you further about the position. Thank you for your consideration and I look forward to hearing from you.

- I welcome the opportunity to discuss with you personally how my skills and strengths can best serve your academy.

- I am very excited to learn more about this opportunity and share how I could contribute to ________________ (company).

Signature:

Here are four signatures that are appropriate for this type of letter.

- Best,
- Regards,
- Sincerely,
- Many thanks,

SAMPLE COVER LETTER : 2

Ji Hye Kim

Daegu, South Korea
+82 10-1234-5678

September 15, 2021
Dear Director Yong,

I was pleased to learn of your need for an English Teacher at Blue Ocean English Academy. I have ample experience using appropriate teaching and assessment methods. I am prepared to become an immediate team player within your organization.

My strong initiative and exceptional organizational skills, combined with my ability to work well under pressure, allow me to play a crucial role in a fast-paced teaching environment. Furthermore, I am capable of simplifying lessons to make sure each student understands the material.

I welcome the opportunity to discuss with you personally how my skills and strengths can best serve your academy.

Sincerely,
Ji Hye Kim

jihye123@gmail.com

COVER LETTER: Practice 1

This is an example cover letter with parts missing. Use your imagination to complete the cover letter. There are no "exact" answers. Use your brain! ☺

Job: Overseas Sales Assistant

Do-hyun Park

Daegu, South Korea
(82) 10-1234-5678 / dohungkim1997@naver.com

Dear Mr. Jung ho Lee,
I was excited to see that _______________ (company) is looking to hire an entry level _________________________ (job title).
I feel that I am good fit for this position because of my strong _________________ (skill: ex: English language, sales, interpersonal skills,…). I have used my language skills as _____________________________ (where? jobs?) Also, I have excellent ______________________ (**skill:** communication, customer service, ….) that will help me get alone with foreign clients. Because of my enthusiasm and ______________, I am confident that I would be a great fit for your company.

I am very excited to learn more about this opportunity and share how I could contribute to _________________ (company).

Sincerely,
Do-hyun Park

COVER LETTER: Practice 2

This is an example cover letter with parts missing. Use your imagination to complete the cover letter. There are no "exact" answers. Use your brain! ☺

Job: Beyond English Academy

Soo Jin Lee

Daegu, South Korea
010-1234-5678

Dear Director Kim,

I am interested in the position as a __________________(job) at ________________ (academy name). I feel my education, as an English major at Yeungnam University, has given me the tools needed to be a good match for your academy.

(the body: write about your experience)

____

____

____

____

I would love the opportunity to speak with you further about the position. Thank you for your consideration and I look forward to hearing from you.

Regards,
Soo Jin Lee
leesoojin@gmail.com

YOUR COVER LETTER: Practice 3

Using your own job posting and resume, practice all the parts of your cover letter.

____

____

____

Dear ________________ (name of contact or hiring manager)

_______________, (signature)

______________________________ (name)

ASSIGNMENT 2: COVER LETTER

1. Chose a template that matches your resume, or a basic letter format.
2. Print _______ copies and bring them to class on Peer Workshop Day.
3. Remember - a cover letter is written to sell yourself, not to simply repeat what is on your resume. This creates the first impression of you.

Peer Workshop Day - first draft due: ______________

Final draft due: ______________

***Print your cover letter and read it out loud to yourself slowly**

COVER LETTER: PEER WORKSHOP

Peer Edited by: ______ (student)	Excellent	Good	Needs improvement	Comments
Appearance/Style/Format Is the letter visually appealing?				
Content/Layout Does the letter have sections such as • Header (name/contact) • Greeting • Introduction • Body • Closing • Signature				
Specific Details/Examples Does the letter highlight some experience in an interesting way?				
Editing/Grammar Is the letter free of errors? What changes/edits need to be made?				
Use of keywords/powerwords Does the letter include keywords from the job posting? Does the letter use any POWERWORDS?				
Details Check and double check ALL fine details of formatting etc.				

COVER LETTER: PEER WORKSHOP

Peer Edited by: (student)	Excellent	Good	Needs improvement	Comments
Appearance/Style/Format Is the letter visually appealing?				
Content/Layout Does the letter have sections such as • Header (name/contact) • Greeting • Introduction • Body • Closing • Signature				
Specific Details/Examples Does the letter highlight some experience in an interesting way?				
Editing/Grammar Is the letter free of errors? What changes/edits need to be made?				
Use of keywords/powerwords Does the letter include keywords from the job posting? Does the letter use any POWERWORDS?				
Details Check and double check ALL fine details of formatting etc.				

UNIT 5

EMAILS:
SUBMITTING APPLICATION DOCUMENTS

Once you have a good resume and cover letter, you're ready to send your documents to a potential employer! You need to think about the email (subject line, greeting, opening/body, closing, and signature), the format of the documents you are sending, and even your email address.

EMAIL ADDRESSES – FIRST IMPRESSIONS

The most popular international email services in the world are

1. Gmail: Gmail is the most used & the best free email service around the globe
2. Outlook.com: Outlook is a famous free email service from Microsoft
3. Yahoo.com: Yahoo mail is another popular free email service

What are the most popular email services in your country?

____

____

____

Tip:

Your email address can say a lot about you. It also gives a first impression to the company. Look at these email address. What is your first impression of the person based on the address?

Kissykissygirl@yahoo.com
Johnattheparty247@gmail.com
2kabakaurt45*r@naver.com
foreverdreaming2001@gmail.com

Write your email here: ____

What kind of impression does it give? Do you need to make a new email address?

Yes / No

PARTS OF AN E-MAIL

1. Address
2. Subject line
3. Greeting
4. Opening / Body
5. Closing
6. Signature

ANALYZE SAMPLE EMAILS

Discuss the following questions with your partner for each of the following samples:

- What is your first impression of each email?
- What are some things that could be improved?

Sample 1:

To: employer@job-postings_company1.co.kr

Subject: Job Application

Dear employer,

Look at my resume and cover letter. It'll tell you all about me. I really want this job.

Thanks,
Ji Sun

ANALYZE SAMPLE EMAILS

Sample 2:

To: sallysmith@gmail.com

Subject: Flight crew

Dear Sally,

Please take care of your health during the cold season. I am writing to apply for flight crew. I know you will find my qualifications meet your requirements.

Contact me at +82 10-4587-9854 (Korea standard time) or at jiyeon2547@naver.com. I want to schedule an interview.

Honorably,

Ji Yeon

Sample 3:

To: jane.doe@starbucks.com

Subject: Job application: Manager, San Francisco branch

Dear Ms. Doe,
My name is Hye Sook Kim, and I'm currently a team leader at the Yeungnam University branch Starbucks, South Korea.

As you can see from my attached resume, I've been working for Starbucks Korea for the last two years and it's been an amazing experience. I have implemented dramatic changes to my team's customer service abilities through an intensive English customer service program that I designed. However, I'm interested in moving to the US and advancing my career into management.

I'd love the opportunity to speak to you about this position further, or to clarify any questions you may have about my experiences or background.

Thank you for your time. I look forward to continuing my career with Starbucks Coffee.

Best,
Hye Sook Kim
+82 10-1234-5678
kimhyesook@yahoo.com

ANALYZE SAMPLE EMAILS

Sample 4:

To: edward.bolton@nike.com

Subject: Internship, Singapore office: Min Su Kim

Dear Edward Bolton,
I am a graduating senior, studying English Language and Literature at Yeungnam University, and I am pleased to present you with my application materials for the marketing internship position.

I have attached my resume, cover letter, and transcripts as requested to this email. If you have any questions or need more information, I can be reached via phone or email.

Thank you for your consideration.

Regards,
Min Su Kim
(123) 456-7890
MinSuKim@gmail.com

PARTS OF AN EMAIL: IN DETAIL

<u>SUBJECT LINE</u>:
Pay attention to what you write in the subject line of an email. Hiring managers receive TONS of emails, so if your subject line is too generic, too long or misspelled, or doesn't give a clear message, your email might not even get opened or be filtered into the trash folder.

- Keep it short
- Be clear about what job you're applying for
- Include your name

PARTS OF AN EMAIL: IN DETAIL

GREETING:

The greeting will start with "Dear" but we need to be careful with titles.

1. Dear (person's name) is the best
   - ✓ Dear Alex Johnson,
2. Dear Mr. or Ms. Last name (Mrs. is not appropriate because you don't know if the female is married or not)
   - ✓ Dear Mr. Johnson,
   - ✓ Dear Ms. Smith,
3. If you don't know the person's name, you can use
   - ✓ Dear Hiring Manager,

- Try to do some research to find out the name of the person you're sending it to - you can try to search the company website or job posting.

OPENING/BODY:

Be specific right away about why you're sending this email. Use formal language. You can mention where you found the job posting (company website, contact person at the company, job search website, etc.)

- I am writing to apply for the ___________ (job)
- I am very interested in applying for the _________ (job) position recently advertised on ___________ (website)
- I would like to express my interest in the _________ (job)

Say what documents you are attaching, and be sure to attach them before you send the email ☺

- Attached are my resume and cover letter, as requested.

Mention the best way to contact you.

- I can be reached at ……. (telephone number, email)

PARTS OF AN EMAIL: IN DETAIL

CLOSING:
Your closing should almost always include a thank you, and be no more than a sentence or two.

- Thank you for your time and consideration.
- I appreciate your taking the time to review my application documents.

SIGNATURE:
Here are four signatures that are appropriate for this type of email:

- Best,
- Regards,
- Sincerely,
- Many thanks,

Some signatures that should be avoided for this type of email:

- Yours truly,
- Respectfully/Respectfully yours,
- Love,
- Best wishes,
- Cheers,
- Take care,
- Thx,
- Always,
- Have a blessed day,

DOCUMENT FORMATTING

.docx is the international standard format for Microsoft Word documents. It's also the most current. However, if you aren't sure, it's best to save and attach your documents as PDFs.

TONE: LANGUAGE SAYS A LOT

When you're writing to make requests of someone in the business world, you should be careful with the tone of your writing. Sometimes, if you say something directly, you might unintentionally sound aggressive, which can make hiring managers feel uncomfortable, or they might get the impression that you are an aggressive person. Using a polite and indirect tone is best.

Direct		Indirect
I want to introduce myself.	➡	I would like to introduce myself.
Send me an email.	➡	Please contact me at your earliest convenience.
Contact me	➡	If you have any questions, I can be reached at…

PRACTICE: Rewrite each of the following sentences from direct to indirect language.

I want to meet you for an interview

____

Contact me now at 010-1234-5678 or at johnjones@outlook.com

____

Look at my resume and cover letter and contact me for an interview.

____

I know you won't regret hiring me.

____

Call me, thanks.

____

Hi, I'm applying for the job.

____

PRACTICE: EDITING

Edit the following email to fix any mistakes in grammar, punctuation, tone, or content as you think is necessary. There are 13 mistakes

TO: Jennifer_Harrison@gmail.com

SUBJECT: Applying for a job

Mr. Harrison,

I am writting to apply for the job posted online. I have plenty of englsih experience, so I will be a perfect person for the job.

Attached are my resume and clover letter, as requested. You can contact me by phone or email.

Take care of yourself not to catch a cold!

Cheers,

Richard

PRACTICE: WRITING

Use the two jobs from Unit 4 (Overseas sales assistant and English teacher at Beyond English Academy) and write an email to submit your documents, and request an interview

1.

TO: ____

SUBJECT: ____

____

____

____

____

____

____

____

____

____

____

2.

TO: ____

SUBJECT: ____

____

____

____

____

____

____

____

____

____

____

ASSIGNMENT 3: SEND AN EMAIL

Due: ___________

Send to: ____________________

For this homework assignment, write an email to request an interview. You must also attach your finalized (fully revised) copies of both your cover letter and resume.

You must pretend this is really going to the hiring manager/contact person for "your" job. As such, your subject line, greeting, content/body, closing, and signature should be written EXACTLY as you would write it to that person.

Subject line: (DON'T include your Korean name or student number here)
Dear ___________ (DON'T address it to me)
BODY OF EMAIL
Signature, (Choose an appropriate signature)
Your Name (in English)

ANSWER KEY

TO: Jennifer_Harrison@gmail.com

SUBJECT: Applying for a job (1. need specific job)

Mr. Harrison, (2. and 3. no greeting and Jennifer is not a Mr.)

I am writting (4.spelling) to apply for the job posted online (5. need name of job). I have plenty of englsih (6. spelling) experience, so I will be a perfect person for the job. (7. too direct)

Attached are my resume and clover (8. spelling) letter, as requested. You can contact me by phone or email. (9. too direct)

Take care of yourself not to catch a cold! (10. culturally inappropriate)

Cheers, (11. and 12. Informal signature and no last name)
Richard
(13. no phone number)

UNIT 6
THE JOB INTERVIEW

WARM-UP AND DISCUSSION:

Talk with your partner or your team.

- Have you ever had a job interview? Tell your partners what happened. (Part-time job interview is ok)
- What are some dos and don'ts for a job interview? Make a list

Dos	Don'ts

- What questions do you think the interviewer might ask? Make a list

- What's the WORST thing that could happen during an interview? Come up with a story of the worst that could happen in an interview.
- What are some of your fears about job interviews?
- What are some of your fears about English interviews?

INTERVIEW QUESTIONS: WARM UP

Here are the TOP TEN interview questions from the internet. (In no specific order, but usually number one is the first question asked)

1. Tell me about yourself.
2. What do you know about our company?
3. What are your greatest strengths or weaknesses?
4. How would you describe yourself in three words?
5. Why should I hire you?
6. Why do you want to work for our company?
7. Describe a time where you had to handle a difficult situation.
8. What do you have to offer our company?
9. What are your future goals?
10. Tell me about your previous work experience?

Warm up:

With a partner - Ask and answer these questions. Try your best! We will learn how to answer these better later.

You may need to use the job from your resume and cover letter to help answer some of the questions.

HOW TO ANSWER QUESTIONS EFFECTIVELY

We never know what questions will be asked in a job interview but we can prepare by practicing some common questions. You will be practicing these questions, as well as some other common questions, with multiple partners, groups, etc. throughout the coming weeks. After all, practice makes perfect ☺

We'll be working on questions from the following categories:

- ✓ Basic
- ✓ Experiences, Company, Career/Future
- ✓ Behavioral
- ✓ Scenario based
- ✓ Conclusion

BASIC QUESTIONS

✓ *Tell me about yourself.*

"Nice to meet you (your name), could you start by telling us a little bit about yourself?" This is a common first question and a very important one. This question is an 'icebreaker.' It allows the interviewer a chance to "get to know you" a little and sets the tone of the interview.

*sets the tone = gives a first impression of you to the people you want to work for

> *Example :*
> *"My name is Kim Min Gyu. I'm 23 years old and a senior at Yeungnam University. I like baseball and hanging out with friends."*

Is this a good answer? No - because this is a job interview, not a blind date ☺

TIP: Don't start your introduction like you're still in elementary school.
Example: ***"My name is Kim Min Gyu. I'm from Daegu. Nice to meet you."*** ☹

TIP: Listen to the interviewer. Did he/she greet you by name when they shook your hand or welcomed you in? If so, there's obviously no need to restate "My name is…"

TIP: If you have a "Western" name that you would like to be called, here is when you can mention it. It's not required.
Example: "My name is Min Gyu, but you can call me James."

A good answer to this question shows how you project yourself, shows that you're articulate, and shows your confidence.

BASIC QUESTIONS

Start with brief information about yourself. You can talk about your major, and/or talk about something interesting related to your experience and why it is important for this job.

> *Example :*
> *"Hi, I'm Min Gyu and I'm a senior at Yeungnam University. I'm studying English Language and Literature, and I expect to graduate in 2021. I worked as a student ambassador for one year and studied abroad for two months in Canada. These experiences inspired me to seek a position in this field."*

ON YOUR OWN

Think of how you would answer "Tell me about yourself." Your answer should be ideally no more than 30 seconds.

PRACTICE

Practice your answer with 3-4 students. The more you practice it, the more natural it should become. Speak naturally. Try to let your personality come through.

✓ What are your greatest strengths and weaknesses?

This is a hard question, right? How's this as for an example? "I'm lazy and late for class but really good at playing online games!" You will never get a job with an answer like this!

Mostly, the interviewer is trying to see how **honest, self-aware,** and **professional** you are. When you answer, you can try to think of either a PERSONALITY TRAIT or a SKILL/HABIT. A good way to answer can be to follow this formula:

Strength + context and story
Weakness + context and story

Here's an example of an answer that discusses a SKILL/HABIT STRENGTH

"I never miss a deadline. I'm highly organized, and I've used this skill to organize people and projects, such as being involved in the English department musical. From that experience, which was two years ago, I learned a lesson about how to be sure everyone knew what to do and when do to it. I spent a lot of time making sure all the members of the musical were comfortable with the schedule and knew where they needed to be. This created a very easy environment for everyone to succeed."

Some common strengths:

- detail-oriented
- patient
- innovative
- motivated
- positive
- energetic
- a team player
- flexible/versatile
- creative
- determined
- passionate
- honest
- hard working
- reliable
- disciplined/focused
- collaborative
- enthusiastic/passionate/driven
- responsible
- dedicated
- focused
- calm

What are your strengths? List three

____

____

____

Here's an example of an answer that discusses a PERSONALITY TRAIT WEAKNESS

> *"I'm naturally shy. In high school and my first few years at university, it stopped me from speaking up. After being a part of a group project in one of my literature classes, I knew I owed it to my team and myself to confidently share my ideas. I decided to work to overcome my shyness by learning public speaking techniques. I learned practical skills around speaking with others and sharing my opinions. Now, in group settings, I am always the first person to start conversations with the quieter students. I know exactly how they feel, and now I can encourage them to overcome their shyness."*

Some common weaknesses:

- disorganized
- not comfortable taking risks
- too focused/lack of focus
- self-critical
- take on too much responsibility
- don't ask for help when I need it
- perfectionis
- shy/not good at public speaking
- competitive

What are your weaknesses? List three

____

____

____

Here are some tips and techniques for handling weakness questions. Any time you are asked to discuss something negative, you should "spin" it in a way that brings it back to being positive.

- ✓Talk about something that is no longer a weakness. Mention how you overcame the weakness and that you have solved similar problems
- ✓Talk about a knowledge-based weakness, which is easily overcome. Mention why this weakness isn't a serious problem and what steps you are actively taking to solve the problem
- ✓Talk about a character flaw that could ultimately be viewed as a positive characteristic

PRACTICE: MAKE NOTES

Practice an answer that focuses on a strength.

Practice an answer that focuses on a weakness.

EXTRAS – BASIC QUESTIONS:

- Tell me about yourself.
- What are your strengths?
- What are your weaknesses?
- What is your biggest achievement?
- How would your colleagues describe you?
- What kinds of decisions do you find most difficult to make?
- How would you describe your work style?
- How do you keep yourself organized?
- If you had to choose one, would you consider yourself a big-picture person or a detail-oriented person?
- Who was your favorite manager/teacher and why?
- What kind of personality do you work best with and why?
- What are three positive things someone would say about you?
- What are three negative things someone would say about you?
- What three character traits would your friends use to describe you?
- Describe yourself in three words.
- What is your greatest fear?
- What is your biggest regret and why?
- What are the qualities of a good leader? A bad leader? Do you think a leader should be feared or liked?

EXPERIENCES, COMPANY, CAREER/ FUTURE

✓ *Tell me about your previous work experience.*

For this type of question, focus on hard and soft skills. The interviewer is trying to get a sense of what you learned in your previous job, not just the tasks you did.

Examples:

Proficient in MS office	Certificate in ……… .
Good communicator	Quick learner
Good at sales	Excellent customer service
Able to give presentations	Good at problem solving

TIP: Think about the information on your resume and/or your cover letter. Here is your chance to go into more detail about your experiences.

Example 1:
"So, when I worked at Vista Coffee, I learned a lot – including how to make all the espresso beverages and how to use and clean the machines. We cleaned our machines at the end of every day to maintain a healthy environment. I got so good at it that my manager asked me to be the one to train all the new employees on this procedure.

Example 2:
"While working at Coffee Tree, I became familiar with how to use the Micros POS system. As a cashier, I was able to take orders in a very fast paced environment and also deal with any questions or complaints. For example, I had a customer once whose drink order was accidentally overlooked and so she'd been waiting a long time but still hadn't received her drink. As soon as I became aware of her issue, I immediately apologized and upgraded her beverage."

EXPERIENCES, COMPANY, CAREER/ FUTURE

Practice with your partner or your team. Make notes below

ABOUT THE COMPANY, JOB, OR INDUSTRY

The following activities are designed to help you answer questions about the company, such as **"What do you know about our company?"** or **"What attracted you to this company?"**

Information Gap:

Form these common questions about companies.

What/ name/ company? →	What's the company's name?
What / founder's / name?	______________________
When / company / founded?	______________________
What / type / company?	______________________
What / yearly/ revenue?	______________________
How / employees/ have?	______________________
Where / company/ headquarters?	______________________
What / company's nationality?	______________________

IN CLASS ACTIVITY:

Choose who is student A and student B. Student A look at page 84. Student B look at page 85. Practice making the questions and answers with your partner.

EXAMPLES:

STUDENT A: What's the company's name?

STUDENT B: The company name is Samsung.

STUDENT A. What type of company is it?

STUDENT B: It's an electronics company.

IN CLASS ACTIVITY:

STUDENT A:

Company's name	Hewlett-Packard (HP)
Founder's name	Bill Hewlett / David Packard
Year company founded	1939
Type of company	Computer hardware/software - IT services
Yearly revenue	$52 Billion (USD)
Number of employees	55,000
Company headquarters	Palo Alto, California
Nationality	USA

Fill in the information about Student B's company

Company's name	
Founder's name	
Year company founded	
Type of company	
Yearly revenue	
Number of employees	
Company headquarters	
Nationality	

IN CLASS ACTIVITY:

STUDENT B:

Company's name	LG
Founder's name	Koo, In Hwoi
Year company founded	1958
Type of company	Electronics good producer
Yearly revenue	18.5 Trillion Won ($16.5 Billion USD)
Number of employees	210,000
Company headquarters	Seoul, South Korea
Nationality	South Korean

Fill in the information about Student A's company

Company's name	
Founder's name	
Year company founded	
Type of company	
Yearly revenue	
Number of employees	
Company headquarters	
Nationality	

IN CLASS RESEARCH:

Before your interview, you need to do some research about the company you are applying to. Every good candidate should know some facts about the place they may work at.

Research your company (the one from your job posting) and find out the information.

Company's name	
Founder's name	
Year company founded	
Type of company	
Yearly revenue	
Number of employees	
Company headquarters	
Nationality	

Use the information above to formulate your answer. Practice your answer and make notes below.

✓ ***What do you know about our company?***

ABOUT YOUR CAREER OR YOUR FUTURE

✓ *What are your future goals?*

This question is focused on the future. No one knows what the future will bring, but this question is NOT about your personal life. The interviewer does not want to hear about buying a car and finding a boyfriend or girlfriend. Answers should be related to work.

Since we don't know the future, we need to be creative. Think about the company and answer the questions in relation to the company.

> *Example 1:*
> *Samsung interview: "I want to learn more about technology and use those skills in the workplace."*
>
> *Airline interview: "I hope to learn about many cultures and use that knowledge to better serve passengers."*

I want to…
I hope to…
I will…
In the next six months… / In the next two years…

Think about the job you want in the future, practice your response to the question. Make notes below

✓ *What are your future goals?*

____

____

____

____

____

EXTRAS – EXPERIENCE, COMPANY, CAREER/FUTURE:

About your experience (university, part-time, volunteer work)

- Why did you choose to study your degree subject?
- What did you most/least enjoy about your time at university?
- What skills did you develop at university?
- How will your degree help you in this position?
- Tell me about your previous work experience.
- Tell me about any volunteer experiences you've had.
- What did you like most/least about your last job?

About the company, job, or industry

- What do you know about our company?
- Why do you want this job?
- What attracted you to this company?
- What can you do for us that other candidates can't?
- What do you consider to be the key skills necessary for this position?
- What would be your ideal working environment?

About your career and your future

- Where would you like to be in your career a year from now?
- How do you hope to develop your career?
- How do you want to improve yourself in the next year?
- What kind of goals would you have in mind if you got this job?

BEHAVIORAL QUESTIONS

Behavioral questions are commonly asked so that the interviewers can predict how you will react, behave, respond, manage, or conduct yourself based on how you have done so in the past.

✓ *Describe a time where you had to handle a difficult situation.*

Example 1:
"When I was working at CU, my coworker was always late, so I couldn't leave on time. I had to talk with my coworker to explain that him being late caused me to be late for class. Instead of telling the manager, I resolved the problem with my coworker and we understood each other's situation."

Example 2:
"During a university class project, our team wasn't working well together. I could see that we needed a clearer plan, so I volunteered to be the leader. I was able to organize all the members on their tasks. As a result, we finished the project early and got a good score."

To structure your answer, it's often easy to follow the SPAR method

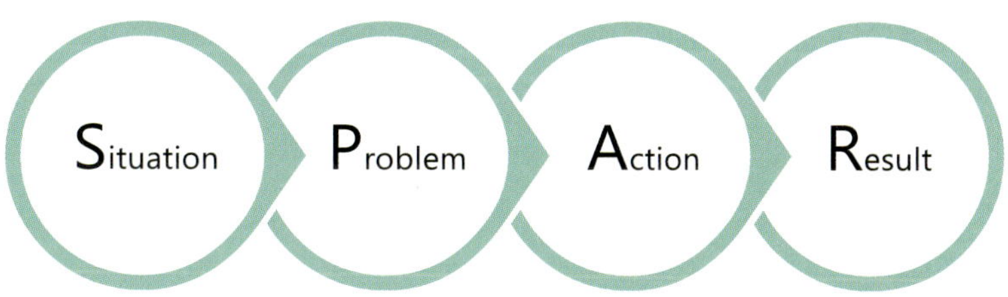

- (S) Situation. Describe the situation in which the event took place.
- (P) Problem. Describe the problem you were trying to solve.
- (A) Action. Explain what action you took to solve the problem.
- (R) Results. Explain the result of your actions. For example, if your actions resulted in solving a problem, resolving a conflict, improving your company's sales record, etc., explain this. Try to focus on how your actions resulted in a success for the company.

BEHAVIORAL QUESTIONS

To prepare for these types of questions, you should be able to recall a story that you have been personally involved in. The stories should fit the following categories (and they can definitely overlap categories)

- Planning
- Teamwork
- Conflict
- Communication
- Making a mistake and fixing it

IN CLASS ACTIVITY

Practice behavioral questions with your partner or group.
"Tell me about a time"…

You had to plan something
You had a conflict with a coworker or classmate
You made a mistake
You communicated well
You were part of a team.

IN CLASS ACTIVITY

EXTRAS – BEHAVIORAL QUESTIONS:

- What was the last project you worked on, and what was the outcome?
- Give me an example of a time that you felt you went above and beyond the call of duty at work.
- Can you describe a time when your work was criticized?
- Have you ever been on a team where someone was not pulling their own weight? How did you handle it?
- How do you handle working with people who annoy you?
- Tell me about a time when you demonstrated good customer service / leadership skills
- Describe a time when you took a risk. What were the results?
- Give me an example of a time you did something wrong. How did you handle it?
- Tell me about a time where you had to deal with conflict on the job.
- Tell me about an assignment that was too difficult for you, and how did you resolve the issue?
- What's the most difficult decision you've made in the last two years and how did you come to that decision?

SCENARIO BASED QUESTIONS

Some companies like to ask questions like "How would you handle…" or "What would you do…" These role-playing questions are designed to see how you would handle difficult scenarios that might happen on the job. These are usually phrased as HYPOTHETICAL questions. Most questions are asking about your skills in the following areas:

- People skills
  (especially handling difficult co-workers, clients, or customers)
- Organizing (especially when under pressure)
- Problem solving
- Communication and persuasion

✓ *"How would you handle a customer who isn't happy with your service even though you've done nothing wrong and they're actually the ones who have made the mistake?"*

Even if the customer is wrong in the scenario, it's not your job to tell the interviewer that. They don't want to hear you say anything negative about the customer; rather, they want to hear how you're going to solve the problem.
The interviewer wants to know you can handle a situation like this if it happens. They want to know that you're calm and can handle the customer with professionalism, even if that customer becomes rude, arrogant, or demanding.

IN CLASS ACTIVITY

Practice scenario based questions with your partner or team.

- You work at an English academy and one student causes a lot of problems in the class. You need to call the mother and explain the situation. What would you say to her?
- You are at the check-in counter for Asiana Airlines. A passenger arrives 20 minutes late for check-in. The flight is going to leave and they can't board the plane. They are really upset. What would you do?
- You work at GS25 and some middle school students come in the store and start stealing snacks. What would you do?
- You have a group presentation at school. One of your group members won't help and doesn't answer text messages. What would you do?
- You work in a company and really like your job, but one co-worker is very rude to you and others in the office. What would you do?

EXTRAS – SCENARIO BASED QUESTIONS:

- If I were your supervisor and asked you to do something that you disagreed with, what would you do?
- If you were interviewing someone for this position, what traits would you look for?
- What would you do if your boss demanded you to work way more hours than you expected?
- What would you do if you were nominated team leader but you weren't prepared or confident for the role?
- How would you handle being asked to move to a different city on short notice?
- How would you handle being pressured to drink during dinner parties, but you don't drink?
- How would you handle a customer who isn't happy with your service even though you've done nothing wrong and they're the ones who made the mistake?
- How you would handle a situation if you were required to finish multiple tasks by the end of the day, and there was no way that you could finish them.

CONCLUSION

So, how does an interview end? Sometimes, an interviewer will directly ask you **"Why should we hire you?"** Other times, he/she might ask **"Do you have any questions for me/us?"** It's good to focus on the reasons why you want the job and the skills you can bring to the job.

TIP: Don't use the same examples or answers that you've already used. This is your chance to leave them with a good final impression.

Here are some examples you can use for the question, "Do you have any questions for me/us?"

- What kind of training do you provide new hires?
- What kind of growth opportunities are there?
- Can you describe a typical day in this type of role?
- How long have you been at the company and what makes you stay?
- How would you describe the work environment and corporate culture?
- What are some of the goals for the company in the short and longer term?
- What would make someone really successful in this role?
- What impact would I have on the team if I get hired?
- What's the one question you really want to ask me but haven't?

FINISHING THE INTERVIEW

When the interview is done, the interviewer will most likely thank you for coming. It's IMPORTANT for you to thank them also. A common closing is like this:

Interviewer: Thanks for coming in today.

Interviewee: Thank you for your time. Hope to hear from you soon.

MOCK INTERVIEW ACTIVITY

Imagine you are the interviewer. Choose seven questions from throughout the chapter. Try to choose questions that move logically from one to the next. Start with a basic introduction question and then continue with more specific questions.

Practice:

1. So, (name) could you tell me about yourself____________________________
2. ____
3. ____
4. ____
5. ____
6. ____
7. ____

Practice: Use different questions.

1. So, (name) could you tell me about yourself____________________________
2. ____
3. ____
4. ____
5. ____
6. ____
7. ____

MOCK INTERVIEW ACTIVITY

Practice: Use different questions.

1. So, (name) could you tell me about yourself____________________________
2. ____
3. ____
4. ____
5. ____
6. ____
7. ____

Practice: Use different questions.

1. So, (name) could you tell me about yourself____________________________
2. ____
3. ____
4. ____
5. ____
6. ____
7. ____

Practice: Use different questions.

1. So, (name) could you tell me about yourself____________________________
2. ____
3. ____
4. ____
5. ____
6. ____
7. ____

UNIT 7

NONVERBAL COMMUNICATION

BODY LANGUAGE SPEAKS LOUDER THAN WORDS

What non-verbal mistakes are being made here? Talk with your partner or group.

READING:

"Is your body language sabotaging your interview?"

Imagine you are perfectly qualified for a job and during the interview you got all the questions right but still didn't get the job offer. Recent studies suggest that your body language is more important than you might think. Studies suggest that only 7% of what you say is important during an interview. Vocal elements like tone and volume are 38% and non-verbal communication make up 55% of the interviewer's decision. What is non-verbal communication? Non-verbal communication is posture, gestures, and facial expressions. Here are some tips that will help you ace your next job interview.

Posture: the way you sit is very important in the way people perceive you. Don't slouch or fold your arms - this makes you look defensive and nervous. It is best to lean forward at the waist and open your arms or have your arms resting on your legs. This will make you look engaged and interested in what the person is saying.

During an interview almost everyone is nervous. Here are some tips to make you look calm and relaxed. One, don't move around in your chair. Moving around and shaking your arms or legs makes you look nervous. Have good posture and sit calmly. Two, don't play with things! Touching your hair, buttons on your shirt, or jewelry will make you look nervous. Also, never play with your smartphone during an interview. Turn it off!

Hand gestures are also important for success. Don't talk wildly with your hands or body movements. Keep your hands open so the palms of your hands can be seen. You can place your hands on your legs or the table. Also, the palm of your hand can give positive or negative signals to an interviewer. An open palm makes people look honest. However, a closed palm or fist can make you look aggressive.

When you look at someone make sure you are engaged. Eye contact is key to gaining trust, but many people do this wrong. Look at the interviewer but don't stare. This can be done by looking at the left eye, right eye, and then chin. Let your eyes move in a triangle. You want your eye contact to be natural and not aggressive. Also, don't look at the ceiling or walls when speaking - this makes you look like you are lying. Have a calm look on your face and SMILE. People like to hire friendly people because they will work with them in the future.

If you follow these tips, I'm sure you will be on your way to a successful interview and career.

ACTIVITIES:

Part A: Match the word with the definition

Engaged _	a. to become aware through the senses
Palm_	b. to destroy or damage something by yourself
Sabotage_	c. inner part of the hand, between the fingers and wrist
Perceive_	d. to look interested or involved
Posture_	e. the position of the body when sitting or standing

Part B: Think and Explain

Look at the expression from the reading. Explain the sentences and demonstrate them with your partners.

"Don't slouch or fold your arms"

"Don't talk wildly with your hands or body movements"

"An open palm makes people look honest. However, a closed palm or fist can make you look aggressive."

"Have a calm look on your face and SMILE."

"Eye contact is key to gaining trust."

Part C: Answer the questions about the reading

What are the percentages for:

- What you say: ______
- Vocal elements: ______
- Non-verbal Communication: _____

Why is it important to have good eye contact?

If you move about in the chair, what does that express?

If you slouch or fold your arms, what does that mean?

When you sit forward and open your arms, how does that make you look?

If you open your palms, what does that make people think?

If you look at the ceiling or walls while talking, what messages does this give?

Part D: Express your opinion:

Why is non-verbal communication ranked at the top?

What are some other non-verbal mistakes people make? Make a list

Why is confidence more important than what you say?

How can people improve their non-verbal skills?

NONVERBAL COMMUNICATION: COMMUNICATING WHAT YOU WANT AND NOT WHAT YOU DON'T WANT

HANDSHAKE

A handshake is one of the first ways you communicate with your interviewer. Your handshake communicates certain things to the person whose hand you are shaking. Avoid these four common mistakes when shaking hands!

- × The "spaghetti arm" handshake: your arm is weak like a spaghetti noodle. This can signify weakness of character
- × The "dead fish" handshake: your hand is too soft and doesn't grip the other person's. This can signify insecurity
- × The "strongman" handshake: your hand is too strong and your handshake is too hard. This can signify arrogance, or that you are trying to dominate the other person.
- × The "long" handshake: your handshake lasts way too long. This tells hiring managers that you might be trying too hard to impress them or that you might not tell the truth.

Practice your handshake as much as possible. Differences in culture can be easily misunderstood, so know your audience! Match his/her level of firmness and length of handshake.

GESTURES

Out of control gestures can take attention away from what you're saying. Too many hand and arm movements can be distracting and can even make you appear more nervous or unsure of what you're saying. Avoid the following:

- × Tapping your foot
- × Shaking your legs
- × Clicking or spinning a pen
- × Touching your hair or face

POSTURE

Pay attention to your body posture during an interview. How you sit can communicate whether you are interested and open, or whether you are nervous or less confident.

- × Don't lean back in the chair
- × Don't cross your arms or your legs

- ✓ Sit up straight, but try to look relaxed
- ✓ Lean slightly forward at the waist

EYE CONTACT

Making eye contact can be uncomfortable at first, but not having the right kind of eye contact could lose you the job you want in an instant. Keep your eye contact casual and relaxed.

- ✓ Try to imagine a triangle on the person's face between their eyes and mouth. Keep your gaze in that area and look at all points

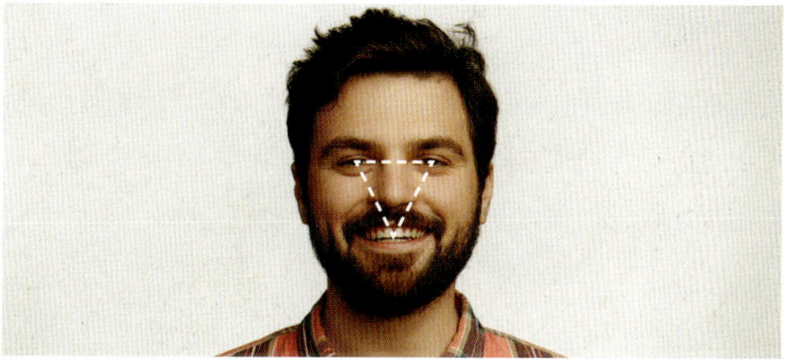

FACIAL EXPRESSIONS

Humans have emotions, so when you don't smile or have any type of positive facial expression during an interview, it can be a turnoff for hiring managers. Try imagining the interview is a typical conversation with a friend - and don't be afraid to show your personality. Really! It's okay to laugh and even make a funny comment every now and then. Hiring managers want to hire real people, not robots.

CLOTHING

It's important to be dressed appropriately for an interview. Wearing formal business clothes is the best option since it's always better to be OVER-dressed than UNDER-dressed in this situation.

For men, formal business clothes includes:

- ✓ Suit (blue, black, or grey)
- ✓ Button-down shirt (dress shirt)
- ✓ Polished dark dress shoes
- ✓ Dark socks that match your pants (No white socks!)
- ✓ Conservative necktie (No sparkles or pictures!)

For women, formal business clothes includes:

- ✓ Suit (blue, black, or grey)
- ✓ Button-down shirt (dress shirt)

SMELLS

Smells can overwhelm a small space! Wearing any kind of perfume, cologne, aftershave, or even overly smelly lotion isn't a good idea under any circumstance. Also, you shouldn't go in to an interview smelling like an ashtray. Hiring managers should remember you, not your smell.

- ✓ No perfume
- ✓ No smelly lotion
- ✓ No cologne/aftershave
- ✓ No cigarette smell

PUTTING IT ALL TOGETHER: MOCK INTERVIEW

Approach this as if it's the REAL thing! You and your partner should begin by standing, shaking hands, sitting down, asking/answering the questions, and then finish with another handshake and a thank you.

1. ______________________________
2. ______________________________
3. ______________________________
4. ______________________________
5. ______________________________
6. ______________________________

1. ______________________________
2. ______________________________
3. ______________________________
4. ______________________________
5. ______________________________
6. ______________________________

1. ______________________________
2. ______________________________
3. ______________________________
4. ______________________________
5. ______________________________
6. ______________________________

Final Exam: Job Interview

Eye contact	Eye contact	Body language	Posture	Overall presence
☺☹				

Verbal:	Ability to answer questions	Listening and interaction	Quality of responses	Language	Overall impression
☺☹					

HIRED? ☺☹

Final Exam: Job Interview

Eye contact	Eye contact	Body language	Posture	Overall presence
☺☹				

Verbal:	Ability to answer questions	Listening and interaction	Quality of responses	Language	Overall impression
☺☹					

HIRED? ☺☹

Final Exam: Job Interview

Eye contact	Eye contact	Body language	Posture	Overall presence
☺☹				

Verbal:	Ability to answer questions	Listening and interaction	Quality of responses	Language	Overall impression
☺☹					

HIRED? ☺☹